Bus Driver

my friendly neighborhood

Published in the United States of America by Cherry Lake Publishing
Ann Arbor, Michigan
www.cherrylakepublishing.com

Reading Adviser: Marla Conn MS, Ed., Literacy specialist, Read-Ability, Inc.
Book Design: Jennifer Wahi
Illustrator: Jeff Bane

Photo Credits: © Monkey Business Images / Shutterstock.com, 5, 9, 13, 23; © Joseph Sohm / Shutterstock.com, 7;
© Michaelpuche / Shutterstock.com, 11; © Africa Studio / Shutterstock.com, 15; © CaseyMartin / Shutterstock.com, 17;
© Claudio Divizia / Shutterstock.com, 19; © Dainis Derics / Shutterstock.com, 21; © aleksandr-mansurov-ru, 2-3, 24;
Cover, 1, 10, 14, 18, Jeff Bane

Library of Congress Cataloging-in-Publication Data has been filed and is available at catalog.loc.gov

Printed in the United States of America
Corporate Graphics

table of contents

About the author: Samantha Bell has written and illustrated over 60 books for children. She lives in South Carolina with her family and pets. She is very thankful for the helpers in her community.

About the illustrator: Jeff Bane and his two business partners own a studio along the American River in Folsom, California, home of the 1849 Gold Rush. When Jeff's not sketching or illustrating for clients, he's either swimming or kayaking in the river to relax.

neighborhood helper

People go many places.
Bus drivers help them get there.

Some drive school buses.
They take students to school.

They take students on field trips. They bring them home after school.

What color is a school bus?

Some bus drivers follow a **route**.
They stop many times.

They pick up people. They drop off people. They help some people get on the bus.

They collect the bus **fare**. People pay with money or tickets.

Some bus drivers take people to another city. The city may be close by. It may be far away. The **passengers** wait at the bus station.

What city would you like to visit?

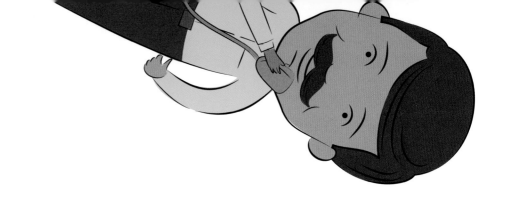

Some drive very large buses.
They take people on trips.

Bus drivers work in all kinds of weather.

They drive when it is sunny.
They drive when it snows.

Bus drivers drive carefully.
They keep the passengers safe.

What would you like to ask a bus driver?

glossary & index

glossary

fare (FAIR) the price paid to ride on a bus, train, or airplane

passengers (PAS-uhn-jurz) people who ride in a vehicle

route (ROOT) a road or way of travel

index